扫描文章前的二维码
收听该故事的英文音频

"伟人的少年故事"丛书

突破障碍的人

―― 改写了科学史的伟大人物 ――

（斯里兰卡）努雷·维塔奇（Nury Vittachi）著
斯泰帕·张（Step Cheung）图
朱之翀 译　张群 审校

上海科技教育出版社

图书在版编目(CIP)数据

突破障碍的人：改写了科学史的伟大人物 /（斯里）努雷·维塔奇（Nury Vittachi）著；朱之翀译 .—上海：上海科技教育出版社，2018.8

("伟人的少年故事"丛书)

书名原文：Women of Discovery

ISBN 978-7-5428-6706-3

Ⅰ.①突… Ⅱ.①努… ②朱… Ⅲ.①科学家—生平事迹—世界—青少年读物 Ⅳ.① K816.1—49

中国版本图书馆 CIP 数据核字（2018）第 069169 号

Contents

Harriet Newell Noyes The Girl Who Found Her Sisters on the Other Side of the World   3

Merit Ptah The First Woman Doctor in History   9

Sophie Germain The Girl Who Had to Hide Behind a Man's Name   15

Anna Komnene The Murderous Princess Who Found Salvation   23

Maria Merian The Bug Hunter Who Dreamed of the Jungle   31

Amalie Emmy Noether The Girl Who Sat at the Back of the Boys-Only Classroom   39

Jabir Ibn Hayyan The True Story of the Philosopher's Stone   46

Isaac Newton The Bullied Boy Who Fought Back   55

Galileo Galilei The Teenager Who Saw the Light   63

Shakuntala Devi What We Learn from the Strange Tale of the Human Computer   71

目 录

哈略特·纽威尔·那夏理 找到另一半地球上的姐妹们的小女孩 3

梅里特·普塔 历史上第一位女医生 9

苏菲·热尔曼 被迫用男子名掩盖身份的女孩 15

安娜·科穆宁娜 得到拯救的恶魔公主 23

玛丽亚·梅里安 向往丛林的昆虫猎人 31

阿玛莉·艾米·诺特 坐在只有男生的教室后排的女孩 39

贾比尔·伊本·哈扬 哲人石的真实故事 46

艾萨克·牛顿 被欺负后还手的男孩 55

伽利略 观察吊灯的年轻人 63

夏琨塔拉·德维 从人脑计算机的神奇传说中得到的收获 71

THE GIRL WHO FOUND HER SISTERS ON THE OTHER SIDE OF THE WORLD

哈略特•纽威尔•那夏理
找到另一半地球上的姐妹们的小女孩

A GIRL AGED 13, sitting in a church in the USA, had a curious feeling. She felt that her destiny was to do something on the other side of the world.

In those days, the 1870s, young women weren't supposed to be interested in travel or work — only in finding a husband.

But the feeling never left Harriet Newell Noyes, and all through her teens and early 20s, she wondered what that special job would be, and what sort of family she would end up with.

When she was 24, she packed her bags and got on a ship to travel to China.

Although she was supposed to be there as a missionary, Harriet had her own **motto**① : "Actions speak louder than words." She would not tell people to live a life of serving others — she would just live such a life herself, and let people see what it was like.

The first thing she realized when she got to Guangzhou was that her sisters in China had it tough. They got very little education. There were many traditions in society that made sure they had no power, and the worst thing of all: their feet were often painfully **bound**② into tiny packages.

She decided that that was her job — she was going to change all this. But how could one woman, from so far away, have any effect?

It seemed impossible.

一个13岁的美国小姑娘坐在一所教堂里，突然产生了一个奇怪的想法。她感觉在冥冥之中，命运将推着她到世界的另一边去做些什么。

　　那时是19世纪70年代，当时的人们认为，年轻女子除非为了物色对象，否则不应该对旅游或工作感兴趣。

　　但哈略特·纽威尔·那夏理（Harriet Newell Noyes）却不那么认为，在整个青少年时期乃至20多岁时，她都一直在思考，自己将要从事一份怎样神奇的工作，她未来的家庭最终会是怎样的。

※※※

　　当她24岁时，她整装待发，乘上了一艘前往中国的船。

　　尽管她当时是作为一名传教士前往中国，但哈略特坚持着自己的座右铭：<u>"事实胜于雄辩。"</u>她没有告诉人们她要过一种为他人服务的生活——她将去过这样一种生活，然后让人们了解这种生活是怎样的。

　　到达广州后，她意识到的第一件事就是中国的姐妹们生活得很艰难。她们几乎没有受过教育，许多传统观念导致她们没有社会地位。而且最糟糕的是：她们的脚被痛苦地裹在很小的鞋子里。

　　她认为她的工作就是——改变这一切。但一个从远方来的女性，要怎么做才能有所成效呢？

　　这看起来是不可能做到的。

---

① **motto**［'mɒtəʊ］*n*. 座右铭、格言、箴言［mottoes 或 mottos］
② **bind**［baɪnd］*vi*. 结合、装订，有约束力、过紧；*vt*. 绑、约束，装订、包扎、凝固［bound，bound，binding］

But Harriet knew that actions speak louder than words, right? So she started small, with a tiny, free school for women called True Light Seminary, the first girls-only college in the city. She started with only six students, but she **persevered**①, and the operation soon began to grow.

If the women had no money, she provided free meals. If they had nowhere to sleep, she gave them bedrooms.

And gently, gently, she persuaded them that foot-binding was a bad thing — and they should unwrap their feet before it was too late.

As the years went by, Harriet's school became a place of **miracles**② — she taught science, mathematics and many other subjects, and the school produced dozens of nurses, more than a hundred doctors, and almost 300 teachers — all female, and all just as good as the men, or better.

The women who unbound their feet told the others how good it felt, and soon, all the women at True Light had normal, healthy feet.

Twenty years after Harriet had started unwrapping the girls' feet, much of Chinese society was discussing the issue. And the government of that period, the Qing Dynasty, passed a law recognizing that feet-binding was evil and was banned forevermore.

Harriet had played a small part in achieving a miracle for her sisters on the other side of the world — and they could all, quite literally, dance for joy.

但哈略特坚信行动胜于空谈，不是吗？所以她从小事做起，建立了第一所叫作真光书院的免费女校。一开始学校只有6名学生，但她坚持了下去，学校的规模很快开始扩张。

学生如果没有钱，她就提供免费的伙食。学生如果没有地方睡觉，她就提供免费的住宿。

逐渐地，她劝说她们，裹小脚是不好的，她们应该在情况变得更糟之前把自己的脚从束缚中解放出来。

一年年过去，哈略特的学校创造了奇迹。她教科学、数学和很多其他科目，学校培养了大量的护士、超过100位医生和将近300位教师。她们都是女性，而且和男性一样优秀，有些甚至超过了男性。

解放了小脚的女性告诉人们这种感觉是多么舒服！很快，真光书院里的所有女性都拥有了一双正常而健康的脚。

在哈略特解放女性小脚20年后，中国大部分人开始讨论这个问题。那时的清朝统治者通过了一条法令，认定裹小脚是罪恶的，从此裹脚这项制度被废除了。

哈略特为另一半地球上的姐妹们创造奇迹贡献了自己的一份力量。确切地说，现在，她的姐妹们终于可以高兴地跳舞了。

---

① **persevere** [pɜːsɪˈvɪə] *vi.* 坚持、不屈不挠、固执己见（在辩论中）。[persevered , persevered, persevering]

② **miracle** [ˈmɪrək(ə)l] *n.* 奇迹、奇迹般的人或物、惊人的事例

THE FIRST WOMAN DOCTOR IN HISTORY

梅里特·普塔
历史上第一位女医生

SOME PEOPLE THINK THAT it's only recently that women have been allowed to become doctors. But historians know that there was already a famous woman doctor in 2700 BC, more than four millennia ago, at the dawn of recorded history.

Her name was Merit Ptah and she lived in Egypt. She is the first named female doctor in history, and may also be the earliest named woman scientist of any kind.

The "Pt" in her name is the same "pt" that you see in the word Egypt. The place name comes from the ancient word Hikuptah, which means "Home of the Soul of Ptah".

Merit Ptah was named after the god Ptah, who is said to have created reality with a thought.

That is kind of cool, because modern scientists say there seems to be some mysterious connection between thoughts (in the form of the taking of **conscious**[1] measurements) and the physical reality of the particles which make up everything. (If you are interested in that idea, look up "measurement problem" and "quantum physics".)

This interpretation of quantum physics indicates that matter seems to be made of ideas, as a famous scientist called Werner Heisenberg said, so perhaps reality really is a thought in the mind of someone. But we don't know if his or her name is Ptah!

How do we know about this early doctor, who lived long before most examples of written history?

有些人可能认为，直至近年来女性才被允许当医生。但历史学家发现，在有记载的历史初期，4000 多年前的公元前 2700 年，就出现过一位著名的女医生。

她名叫梅里特·普塔（Merit Ptah），居住在埃及。她是历史上第一位有名字记载的女医生，甚至可能是最早有名字记载的女科学家（所有科学领域中）。

她名字中的"Pt"就是单词"Egypt"（埃及）中的"pt"，Egypt 这个地名来自古单词"Hikuptah"，意为"普塔灵魂之所"。

梅里特·普塔以普塔神的名字命名，据说普塔神在一念之间创造了现实。

这听起来有一点炫酷，因为现代科学家认为，思维（采用意识测量的形式）和组成物质的粒子的物理实体（如果你对这点感兴趣，可搜索"测量问题"和"量子物理"）之间似乎存在着某种神秘的联系。

正如一位名叫海森伯（Werner Heisenberg）的著名科学家所说的，这种关于量子物理的解释似乎表明物质是由思想组成的。所以现实很可能就是某个人大脑中的思维，但我们不知道他 / 她的名字是不是叫作普塔！

在有文字记载的历史长河中，这位早期医生生活的年代要比大多数名人早得多，我们是怎么知道她的呢？

① **conscious** [ˈkɒnʃəs] *adj.* 意识到的、故意的，神志清醒的

A picture of her was found in a tomb in a pyramid, with a piece of text written by her son, a High Priest. He says his mother is "the Chief Physician", which suggests that she was a top doctor with others under her command.

Merit Ptah's existence shows that even in the early days of human history, women could have really important jobs, as they should.

She's important — so in modern times, when astronomers were looking for names to use on landmarks on other planets, they gave her name to a **crater**[1] on the planet Venus, calling it the Merit Ptah crater.

If you grow up to be an inter-planetary explorer, and end up on the planet Venus, I hope you'll remember this tale. You'll be able to tell your friends: "This crater is named after Merit Ptah, the earliest named female scientist in history."

有关她的一幅画在一座金字塔的坟墓中被发现，还附有她的大祭司儿子写下的一段文字。他说他的母亲是"首席医师"，这表明她是一位一流的医生，其他人都要听从她的指挥。

梅里特·普塔的存在证明，即使在人类历史早期，只要有能力，女性也可以担任重要的职位。

她是个重要人物，因此在现代，当天文学家为其他行星上的地标征集名字时，他们用梅里特的名字命名了金星上的一座环形山，将之称为梅里特·普塔环形山。

如果你长大后成为一名行星探险家，并且最终到达了金星，我希望你会记起这个故事。你可以告诉你的朋友："这里有一座环形山是以梅里特·普塔的名字命名的，她是历史上最早的有名字记载的女科学家。"

---

① **crater** [ˈkreɪtə] *n.* 火山口、弹坑；*vt.* 在……上形成坑，取消，毁坏；*vi.* 形成坑、消亡

THE GIRL WHO HAD TO HIDE BEHIND A MAN'S NAME

苏菲·热尔曼
被迫用男子名掩盖身份的女孩

SOPHIE WAS FORBIDDEN from leaving the house. Again! Not fair. For weeks, she had been made to stay indoors.

Why? Sophie Germain, aged 13, lived in a country and a time where bad government had made many people angry. There was fighting in the streets, so she had to stay inside for safety. **Boring**[①]!

What could she do? This was in France in 1789, so there were no computers or Internet or television or any such modern **entertainments**[②] — not even a radio.

But there was one bright spot in her life. Her father had created a library in his house — and she made herself at home in the room full of books, and was soon lost in her own, an armchair traveler in a world of words.

You'd think her parents would be happy, but no. They expected Sophie Germain to read "girl" books, educational ones about art and music and languages.

But Sophie went straight for what her family considered "boy" books, and her favorites were the most unlikely ones of all (so her parents thought): those on mathematics.

She was particularly **enchanted**[③] by reading about Archimedes. He was a Greek mathematician, and many of the important equations we use to build everything from bridges to buildings came from him. A lot of people don't realize that without maths we would not have anything that is engineered — no buildings, no machines, no computers.

苏菲被禁止离开屋子。第二次了！这不公平。好几个星期，她被迫待在房间里。

为什么会这样？13 岁的苏菲·热尔曼（Sophie Germain）住在乡下，当时的政府很糟糕，导致人民非常不满，大街上经常发生争斗。为了安全起见，苏菲不得不待在家里。那是多么的无聊！

她能做什么呢？当时是 1789 年的法国，没有电脑、网络、电视机和任何现代化的娱乐工具——甚至连收音机都没有。

但她的生活中有一个亮点。她的父亲在家里建了一个图书室，苏菲在堆满了书的房间里感到十分自在，很快便沉浸在书的海洋里。她坐在扶手椅上，在文字的世界里旅行。

你可能会认为她的父母会因此很开心，但实际上没有。他们希望苏菲读一些"女性化"的书，比如关于音乐、艺术和语言的有教育意义的书。

但苏菲选择的却是她的家庭所认为的"男性化"的书，她最喜欢的书是所有书里面最不可能被人喜欢的一种（她的父母这样认为）：关于数学的书。

她尤其着迷于阅读关于阿基米德的内容。阿基米德是一位希腊数学家，我们现在设计建造大桥、高楼等建筑物所用到的大部分重要公式都来源于他。很多人没有意识到，如果没有数学，我们就不可能拥有任何需要设计才出现的东西——不会有房屋、机器和电脑。

---

① **boring** [ˈbɔːrɪŋ] *adj.* 无聊的、令人厌烦的
② **entertainment** [ˌentəˈteɪnmənt] *n.* 娱乐、消遣、款待
③ **enchant** [ɪnˈtʃɑːnt; en-] *vt.* 使迷惑、施魔法

One of the history books said that when a Roman soldier killed Archimedes in a battle, the old mathematician's last words referred to the geometry papers he was carrying — "Do not disturb the circles." Mathematics is important!

On dark winter evenings, Sophie would go to her bedroom and stay up late writing equations. Her parents were angry, and took away her room-heater and her coats, so that she would be too cold to work.

Sophie wrapped her blanket around her and worked on the equations she was learning by candlelight.

One morning, her mother found her asleep at her desk on a day so cold that the ink had frozen in her **inkwell**①.

From that time on, her mother secretly helped her.

Sophie Germain grew up to become a great mathematician, although she signed much of her work using a male name "Monsieur LeBlanc".

She made important progress on a very famous puzzle called **Fermat's Last Theorem**②, which had mathematicians around the world **stumped**③.

One of her great achievements was to create a formula to work out the **elasticity**④, or bendiness, of materials. This meant that engineers could build high structures without fearing that they would break into pieces.

一本历史书上说，一位罗马士兵在一场战争中杀死了阿基米德，而这位年迈数学家的最后一句话与他拿着的几何学论文有关："不要动我的圆。"数学是多么重要啊！

在冬季的寒夜，苏菲会在卧室里熬夜写方程。她的父母很生气，把她房间里的加热器取走，还带走了她的外套，以为这样她就会因为太冷而不这么干了。

苏菲把毯子裹在身上，借着烛光继续研究她正在学习的方程。

一天早晨，母亲发现她趴在桌子上睡着了。那天很冷，连墨水池里的墨水都结成冰了。

从那时起，母亲开始悄悄地帮助她。

成年后的苏菲·热尔曼成了一名优秀的数学家，尽管她的大多数工作都是以一个男子名"勒布朗"发表的。

她在费马大定理这个难倒了全世界数学家的问题上取得了重大进展。

她的另一项巨大成就是提出了一个公式，可用于计算物体的弹性。这意味着工程师可以建造高层建筑而不用担心它是否会断裂。

---

① **inkwell** [ˈɪŋkwel] n. 墨水池
② **fermat's Last Theorem** 费马大定理
③ **stump** [stʌmp] vt. 砍伐, 使为难、在……作巡回政治演说; vi. 笨重地行走、发表竞选演说
④ **elasticity** [elæˈstɪsɪtɪ; iː-; ɪ-] n. 弹性、弹力、灵活性 [elasticities]

After her death, the **Eiffel Tower**[1] was built, partly using her calculations. The builders wrote the names of 72 scientists on the tower, but did not put her name on the list, probably because she was a woman.

Next time you see a picture of the Eiffel Tower in France, remember the girl whose name is not on it: the girl who had to stay at home every night — but then discovered her father's library and started traveling in her mind.

苏菲去世后，埃菲尔铁塔建成，而其修建工作也部分使用了她的计算结果。铁塔上铭刻了 72 位科学家的名字，但她的名字却不在其列。可能因为她是位女性吧。

下次看到法国埃菲尔铁塔的照片时，请记住这个名字不在其上的女孩：她不得不每晚待在家中，后来她发现了父亲的图书室，随即她的思想开始遨游其中。

① **Eiffel Tower** 埃菲尔铁塔（位于法国巴黎塞纳河南岸）

THE MURDEROUS PRINCESS WHO FOUND SALVATION

安娜·科穆宁娜
得到拯救的惡魔公主

DID YOU HEAR ABOUT the evil princess who tried to kill her brother?

True story: Once there was a girl called Anna of Byzantium, aged 14. More than anything, she wanted to make history.

She seemed to be in a good position to do so, as she had been born into one of the richest and most powerful families in the **Mediterranean**[①].

But in those days, and this was almost 1,000 years ago, being a princess was tough. Princesses were used as tools to join families together.

While she was a baby, a husband had been chosen for her. But he died while she was still a child.

※※※ ※※※

When Anna (full name Anna Komnene) was 14, another husband was chosen for her: a young leader named Caesar Nikephoros Bryennios the Younger. She agreed — no choice, really. (The two of them seemed to get on well, and eventually had four children.)

But Anna was ambitious and hardworking, and her parents allowed her to be educated in astronomy, mathematics, and (her favorite subject) philosophy, which her teacher said was "the queen of all sciences".

When she became a young woman, her father put her in charge of a hospital, where she learned about life and death and thousands of different types of medicine. She became quite the scientist.

你有没有听说过想要杀死自己弟弟的恶魔公主？

这是一个真实的故事：拜占庭时期，曾经有一个名叫安娜的 14 岁女孩，她想要创造历史，这个欲望超过了一切。

她的身份似乎使她有能力这样做，因为她出生于地中海最富有、最有权势的家庭。

但在差不多 1000 年前的时候，当一位公主并不容易，公主会被作为联姻的工具。

当安娜还是个婴儿的时候，她的丈夫就已经选定了。但她还是个孩子时，丈夫就去世了。

安娜·科穆宁娜（Anna Komnene）14 岁时，她的另一位丈夫被选定了：他是位年轻领袖，名叫小恺撒·尼基弗鲁斯·布里恩尼乌斯（Caesar Nikephoros Bryennios the Younger）。她别无选择，同意了。（他俩似乎相处得还好，最终生了四个孩子。）

但安娜有着雄心壮志，而且非常努力，她的父母允许她学习天文学、数学和老师口中的"科学皇后"——哲学（这是她最喜欢的学科）。

当她成年后，她的父亲让她管理一家医院，在那里她懂得了生老病死，了解了数千种不同功效的药物。她对科学已了如指掌。

---

① **Mediterranean** [ˌmɛdətəˈreɪniən] *n.* 地中海；*adj.* 地中海的

But when her father had more children, and one was a boy, **sexism**① **reared**② its ugly head. It was decreed that he should become the next leader of the land, because even though she was the oldest child, she was just a girl.

And when her dad died, that's what happened.

Anna felt strongly that she and her husband should become the leaders. So she set up a **plot**③ to kill her own younger brother.

But to her amazement, her husband refused to help, and eventually the plot was exposed. Her younger brother, who was now king, took away all the land and money belonging to his sister and her husband and **exiled**④ them.

Anna **complained**⑤ that since women were supposed to be softer-hearted than men, God must have accidentally given her and her husband each other's genders!

Then her luck turned even worse.

Her husband died, and she had nowhere to go except to a **convent**⑥ where she would live as a nun until she died.

It seemed like really bad news — but it turned out to be the best thing that could have happened.

但当她的父亲有了别的孩子，并且其中一个是男孩的时候，性别歧视产生了。那个男孩被任命为这片土地的下一任统治者，原因是：虽然安娜是最年长的孩子，但她是个女孩。

她的父亲去世后，这一切便发生了。

安娜坚信她和她的丈夫应该成为掌权者，所以她密谋杀死自己的弟弟。

但令她惊讶的是，她的丈夫拒绝帮助她。最终这个计划暴露了。她尚未登上王位的弟弟夺走了所有属于安娜和她丈夫的土地和金钱，并且流放了他们。

安娜抱怨道，自从认定女性比男性心软后，上帝一定不小心把她和她丈夫的性别搞反了！

她的运气变得越来越差。

她的丈夫去世了。她无处可去，只能去女修道院做一名修女，直到去世。

这听上去像个坏消息——但最终成就了一件最好的事。

---

① **sexism** ['seksɪz(ə)m] *n.* （针对女性的）性别歧视、男性至上主义
② **rear** [rɪə] *vt.* 培养、树立、栽种；*vi.* 暴跳、高耸
③ **plot** [plɒt] *vt.* 密谋、绘图、划分、标绘；*vi.* 密谋、策划、绘制 [plotted, plotted, plotting]
④ **exile** ['eksaɪl; 'egz-] *n.* 流放、充军、放逐、被放逐者、流放犯；*vt.* 放逐、流放、使背井离乡 [exiled, exiled, exiling]
⑤ **complain** [kəm'pleɪn] *vi.* 投诉、发牢骚、诉说；*vt.* 抱怨、控诉
⑥ **convent** ['kɒnv(ə)nt] *n.* 女修道院

As a nun, living in a quiet place where she could think about the important things in life, she finally became a person of worth. Her life, full of rich and powerful experiences, and all that time she had spent in a hospital, and the **twists** [1] and turns of her life, meant that she had acquired a measure of wisdom.

At the age of 55, she decided to finish writing a book of history and science that her husband had started. It ended up as a 15-volume book called "The Alexiad", containing important knowledge about that period of history, a time in Europe sometimes known as "the dark ages".

Anna of Byzantium, the evil princess who tried to murder her brother, became a good nun and an early science writer — and finally found herself a place in history.

作为一名修女，安娜住在一个安静的场所，在那里她可以思考人生中重要的事。她最终成为了一个有价值的人。她的人生充满了丰富和难忘的经历，她在医院度过的时光和她一波三折的人生都意味着她充满智慧。

在55岁时，她决定将丈夫曾经着手写的一本关于历史和科学的书写完。最终完成的《阿莱克修斯传》有15卷，包含了欧洲历史上那段被称为"黑暗时期"的重要信息。

拜占庭时期想要谋杀弟弟的恶魔公主安娜，成为一名善良的修女和一名早期的科学作家，最终在历史上获得了自己的一席之地。

---

① **twist** [twɪst] *vt.* 捻、拧、扭伤；*vi.* 扭动、弯曲

THE BUG HUNTER WHO DREAMED OF THE JUNGLE

玛丽亚·梅里安
向往丛林的昆虫猎人

GIRLS DON'T LIKE BUGS, RIGHT? Wrong! The truth is that one of the world's greatest bug scientists was a woman. And she started young.

Maria Merian was 13 when she started painting insects. She was particularly intrigued that ugly creatures that looked like horrible **maggots**① could turn into beautiful butterflies.

It was an odd interest for a girl in those days, but she loved knowledge. Her father had been a publisher, so she had been born into a house of books, in 1647 in the city of Frankfurt, Germany.

But he had died when she was three.

Then her mother married a painter, and the child learned to paint from watching her **stepfather**②.

She soon realized that she could combine her interest in insects with her father's skill in book production and her stepfather's skill in painting to create books of nature pictures.

But how could she get people interested in **bugs**③?

She knew what to do — she would have to travel to an exotic distant jungle and find GIANT bugs — insects so big and **scary**④ that they could eat birds!

But of course, real life is never as exciting as your dream, is it? Her life took a rather boringly normal path. Maria Merian grew up, got married, and had children — and would sometimes **sigh**⑤. Would she ever get a chance to make her dream come true?

女孩都不喜欢昆虫,对吗?不!事实上,世界上最伟大的昆虫科学家中,有一名就是女性!她很早就开始研究昆虫。

玛丽亚·梅里安(Maria Merian)13 岁时开始画昆虫。她对看起来像蛆一样的丑陋生物最终能变成美丽的蝴蝶这一点尤其感兴趣。

在那个年代,这对于女孩来说是一个古怪的兴趣,但梅里安酷爱求知。她的父亲是一名出版商,1647 年,她出生于德国法兰克福的一个书香门第。

但梅里安三岁时,她的父亲就去世了。

她的母亲再嫁给了一位画家,梅里安通过观察继父工作学会了画画。

梅里安很快意识到,她可以将自己对于昆虫的兴趣和父亲出书的能力、继父绘画的能力结合起来,创作出自然类的图画书。

但怎么让人们对昆虫感兴趣呢?

她知道该怎么做:去国外遥远的丛林中寻找大型昆虫——大到能够吃下各种鸟的可怕昆虫!

然而,现实不会和梦想一样令人激动,对吧?现实中的梅里安走上了一条相对无聊且正常的人生道路。玛丽亚·梅里安长大了,结婚,生子……她有时会叹气,自己还有没有机会梦想成真呢?

---

① **maggot** [ˈmæɡət] *n.* 蛆
② **stepfather** [ˈstepfɑːðə] *n.* 继父
③ **bug** [bʌɡ] *n.* 臭虫、小虫,故障,窃听器;*vt.* 烦扰、打扰,装窃听器;*vi.* 装置窃听器 [bugged, bugged, bugging]
④ **scary** [ˈskeərɪ] *adj.* (事物)可怕的、恐怖的、吓人的、(人)提心吊胆的、引起惊慌的、胆小的
⑤ **sigh** [saɪ] *vi.* 叹息、叹气;*vt.* 叹息、叹气

One day, she decided that she had to go back to her original dream, and she made the break. She sold 255 of her paintings to raise money, and then set sail on a ship to do a scientific investigation of the insects of a land called Suriname, which is in South America.

She took with her one of her children, 19-year-old Dorothea, plus her notebooks and paints.

Some people say that her trip might be the first real science-focused expedition. (Before that, scientists just took a cabin on ships transporting goods or tourists.)

After weeks of travel, Maria Merian and her daughter entered the jungles of Suriname. They saw lots of amazing things and discovered new animals and plants. Maria painted a **spider**[1] so big that it could capture and eat a bird — something that would amaze her readers, who could never have imagined such a thing.

They spent two years there before returning to Europe. Maria produced lots of paintings and books. One of them, published after her death, was called "The **Caterpillars**[2]' Marvelous Transformation and Strange **Floral**[3] Food".

有一天，她决定回到最初的起点，为梦想稍作停留。为了筹钱，她卖掉了自己的255幅画作，然后登上船，向南美洲的苏里南岛扬帆起航，去那里对昆虫进行科学考察。

她带上了笔记本、颜料和她的一个孩子，19岁的多罗茜亚（Dorothea）。

有人认为，她的这次旅行可能是世界上第一次真正的科学远征。（在此之前，科学家仅仅坐过用于运送货物或者旅客的小船。）

在几周的旅行后，玛丽亚·梅里安和她的女儿进入了苏里南岛的丛林中。她们看到了许多惊人的事物，发现了新的动植物。玛丽安画下了一只巨型的能够捕捉乃至吞噬鸟类的蜘蛛——这将会让她的读者大吃一惊，因为他们从未想象过会存在这样的动物。

她们在那里度过了两年，然后返回欧洲。玛丽亚·梅里安出版了许多画册和图书。其中一本名为《毛毛虫的非凡转变与奇怪的花类食物》，在她去世后出版。

① **spider** [ˈspaɪdə] *n.* 蜘蛛、设圈套者、三脚架
② **caterpillar** [ˈkætəpɪlə] *n.* 毛虫、履带车；*adj.* 有履带装置的
③ **floral** [ˈflɔːr(ə)l; ˈflɒ-] *adj.* 花的、植物的、植物群的、花似的

Have you seen any of those famous BBC TV documentaries about animals? The man who made those, David Attenborough, said Maria Merian was one of the world's most important **naturalists** ① in the area of small creatures.

And recently, on what would have been her 366th birthday, Google dressed up its search page with a Merian-style picture of a young **iguana** ② (its tail made the second "g" in Google).

So don't let anyone tell you that girls can't cope with bugs! Maria Merian introduced the world to some of the biggest and scariest bugs of all.

你有没有看过英国广播公司（BBC）著名的关于动物的电视纪录片？这些纪录片的节目制作人戴维·艾登堡（David Attenborough）说，在小型生物领域，玛丽亚·梅里安是世界上最重要的博物学家之一。

最近，在她诞辰 366 年即将到来之际，为了纪念她，Google 用一幅梅里安画风的小鬣蜥蜴图片装点了自己的搜索主页（小鬣蜥蜴的尾巴构成了 Google 里的字母"g"。）

所以不要再听别人说女孩子对付不了昆虫了！玛丽亚·梅里安就曾向全世界介绍过一些最大、最可怕的昆虫。

---

① **naturalist** [ˈnætʃ(ə)rəlɪst] n. 自然主义者、博物学家、（英）动物标本剥制者、买卖玩赏动物的商人

② **iguana** [ɪˈɡwɑːnə] n. 鬣蜥蜴

THE GIRL WHO SAT AT THE BACK OF THE BOYS-ONLY CLASSROOM

阿玛莉·艾米·诺特
坐在只有男生的教室后排的女孩

CAN YOU BELIEVE IT? She was banned from university for being a girl.

But they let her sit at the back of lectures and listen.

Amalie Emmy Noether listened and learned, and started writing her own scientific **theorems**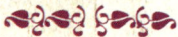 and mathematics formulas.

And would you believe it? They won her a place in history. Albert Einstein, who is often described as one of the smartest people who ever lived, called her "a genius".

And what about the men who worked so hard to keep her out of university? They have all been forgotten!

⁂

Miss Noether was born in 1882 in Germany. She liked to be called Emmy.

She was clever and friendly, but had bad eyesight (she wore thick glasses) and spoke with a bit of a **lisp** ② (which is when your "s" sounds like "th", so you might say "toatht" when you want to say "toast").

In those days, girls were expected to do only a bit of studying, limited to music and languages and dancing, and, of course, cooking and cleaning. Only boys were allowed to take long courses in serious subjects such as math, science and engineering.

But when an adult challenged the children to a brain-teaser at a children's party, he was surprised to notice that it was a little girl, Emmy, who solved it much faster than any of the boys.

你能相信吗？因为她是个女孩，所以被大学拒绝了。

不过他们允许她坐在教室的后排听课。

就这样，阿玛莉·艾米·诺特（Amalie Emmy Noether）一边听一边学习，写下了她自己的科学定理和数学公式。

你相信吗？这些定理和公式让她在历史上占有了一席之地。爱因斯坦常常被描述为有史以来世界上最聪明的人之一，就连他也称赞诺特为"一名天才"。

而那些竭力反对她进入大学的男性怎么样了呢？他们全都被人们遗忘了！

❧❧❧

诺特小姐 1882 年出生在德国，她喜欢被人称作艾米。

她既聪明又友善，但视力不好（戴着厚厚的眼镜片），说话有一些口齿不清（比如"s"的发音像"th"，所以她说"toast"时，听起来像是在说"toatht"）。

在那个年代，人们认为女孩用不着学太多东西，只要学一点音乐、语言、舞蹈，还有厨艺和清洁方面的知识就够了。只有男孩才被允许花时间研读重要的学科，比如数学、科学和工程学。

然而，在一个孩子们的聚会上，当一名成年人跟孩子们比赛玩智力题时，他惊讶地发现，艾米这个小女孩答题的速度超过了任何一个男孩！

---

① **theorem** ['θɪərəm] *n.* 定理、原理
② **lisp** [lɪsp] *n.* 口齿不清、咬舌发音；*vi.* 咬舌讲话、说话口齿不清；*vt.* 咬着舌说、口齿不清地说

When Emmy was a teenager, she took exams in French and English and was expected to become a language teacher. That was allowable for a girl.

But instead, she chose to continue her studies, going to university — despite the fact that universities were strictly for boys only.

The university bosses were not happy. They said that having girls studying "would **overthrow**① all academic order".

Eventually they said she could sit at the back and listen, if she got **permission**② from each lecturer in advance. So she did.

When she finished studying, she got a job as a teacher at a university — but because she was a woman, she had to work for no pay. She did that for seven years.

Some people realized how smart she was, and two professors invited her to join a mathematics department at a university. The other professors complained that women should not be professors. One said: "What will our soldiers think when they return to the university and find that they are required to learn at the feet of a woman?"

So she spent four years giving math lectures using the name of one of her male **colleagues**③.

十几岁时，艾米参加了法语和英语考试，人们期待她成为一名语言教师。这是允许女性从事的职业。

但她却选择继续学习，去上大学——尽管大学非常严苛，只对男性开放。

大学的管理者们很不开心。他们认为让女孩学习"会颠覆所有的学术秩序"。

最终，他们说，如果艾米能够在课前得到教师的准许，她可以坐在教室的后排听课。艾米这样做了。

完成学业后，艾米在一所大学得到了一份教师的工作。但因为她是女性，她的工作没有薪酬。这份工作她做了七年。

有些人发现她非常聪明。有两名教授邀请她加入一所大学的数学系，但其他教授抱怨说女性不能当教授。有一名教授说："当我们的士兵返回到大学时，发现他们必须向一个女人学习，他们会怎么想？"

所以艾米借用了一名男同事的名字，教了四年的数学课。

---

① **overthrow** [ˌəʊvəˈθrəʊ] *n.* 推翻、倾覆、瓦解；*vt.* 推翻、打倒、倾覆［overthrew, overthrown, overthrowing］

② **permission** [pəˈmɪʃ(ə)n] *n.* 允许、许可

③ **colleague** [ˈkɒliːɡ] *n.* 同事、同僚［colleagues］

She kept doing what she was good at, and became famous for one particular discovery.

When we study physics at a deep level, we find intriguing **symmetries**[1] which give rise to laws of **conservation**[2], she said. No one had ever noticed that, or proved it scientifically before. "This concept's played a greater part in physics than relativity and quantum theory," said a report in New Scientist magazine.

Thanks to what Emmy and other women proved, girls are welcomed to study math, science, engineering, and all the other technical subjects that used to be for boys only. And you know what? They are not always as good as the boys. Sometimes, as in Emmy's case, they are better!

And if anyone doubts that, tell them about the young woman who even Einstein looked up to.

她继续做着自己擅长的事，后来因为一项特别的发现而名闻天下。

她说，当深入学习物理后，我们可以发现，奇妙的对称导致人们发现了守恒定律。以前从未有人注意到这一点，也没有人科学地证明过它。《新科学家》杂志的一篇报道评价说："这一观点在物理学上所起的作用，超过了相对论和量子论。"

由于艾米和其他女性作出的榜样，以前只对男性开放的技术类科目，如数学、科学、工程学等，开始欢迎女性加入。你知道吗？女性不仅同男性一样优秀，有时，正如艾米的例子所证明的，女性比男性更优秀！

如果有任何人对此表示怀疑，跟他们讲讲这个连爱因斯坦都尊敬的年轻女子的故事吧！

① **symmetry** [ˈsɪmɪtri] n. 对称(性)、整齐、匀称 [symmetries]
② **conservation** [ˌkɒnsəˈveɪʃ(ə)n] n. 保存、保持、保护

THE TRUE STORY OF THE PHILOSOPHER'S STONE

贾比尔·伊本·哈杨
哲人石的真实故事

FOR MORE THAN 2,000 YEARS, storytellers told tales of wizards and the legend of "the **philosopher's stone**[①]".

You may have heard of this — in the very first Harry Potter book and movie, junior wizard Harry learns about a 655-year-old "alchemist", a type of wizard, who lives in a forest with the "original" philosopher's stone.

(In some places, the book title was changed to "Harry Potter and the Sorcerer's Stone" because publishers were scared that young people would find the word "philosopher" boring compared to the word "sorcerer".)

But the same magical substance appears in many other books and stories, long before it was used by the writer of the Harry Potter stories, J.K. Rowling.

No one knows who was the original storyteller who came up with the idea of the magical stone which could turn ordinary metal into gold or silver, or bring things to life.

❧❧❧ §❧❧❧

Islamic scholars from the 8th century **onwards**[②] may have been the first, or among the first, who started to work out how such things might actually be able to happen.

A man in Persia (modern-day Iran) named Jabir ibn Hayyan said that one metal could be "**transmuted**[③]" into another by rearranging the elements of which it was made.

说书人讲述巫师的故事和"哲人石"的传说，这一历史已经长达2000多年。

　　你可能已经听说过哲人石的故事，在最早关于哈利·波特（Harry Potter）的书和电影中，少年巫师哈利认识一位住在森林里的655岁的"炼金术士"，他有一块"最早的"哲人石。

　　（在一些地区，关于哈利·波特的这本书的书名被改为《哈利·波特与魔法石》，因为出版商担心，年轻人会认为"哲人"这个词比"魔法师"枯燥无味。）

　　但早在作者罗琳（J. K. Rowling）在书中提到哲人石之前，"哲人石"这一神奇的物质就已出现在很多书籍和故事中了。

　　没有人知道，是谁第一个提出神奇石头（哲人石）这一概念的：这种石头能够将普通的金属转变为金子或银子，或者赋予物体以生命。

✦✦✦

　　从8世纪开始，穆斯林学者就一直研究这种变化究竟是如何发生的，他们可能是最早（或之一）搞这种研究的人。

　　波斯（如今的伊朗）有一个叫贾比尔·伊本·哈扬（Jabir ibn Hayyan）的男子说，一种金属可以通过重组其所含的元素"变化"成另一种金属。

---

① **philosopher's stone** 哲人石，炼金术士认为能够将贱金属变为金子的石头或物质
② **onward** [ˈɒnwəd] *adj.* 向前的、前进的；*adv.* 向前、在前面
③ **transmute** [trænzˈmjuːt; trɑːnz-; -ns-] *vt.* 使变形、使变质；*vi.* 变形、变质 [transmuted, transmuted, transmuting]

What substance would make this happen? He didn't know, but he used the Arabic word al-iksir for it. From this term comes the modern word "elixir", which means magic potion — and is another word that we find in the Harry Potter stories, and many other tales about magic, older than those tales.

~~~~~~

For most of the past few centuries, scientists were **skeptical**① about any method of changing one element into another, and said that transmutation was impossible.

They said that stories about alchemists, or wizards, were "unscientific".

Then, in 1901, two British scientists were working in a laboratory on **radioactive**② metals. One of them, Frederick Soddy, noticed that one substance, **thorium**③, was changing into another one, radium.

He called out to his partner, Ernest Rutherford. "Rutherford, this is transmutation!"

Rutherford replied: "Don't call it transmutation. They'll have our heads off as alchemists."

Rutherford was worried that other scientists would identify them as **would-be**④ wizards and they would be disrespected.

It didn't happen. Rutherford and Soddy became famous. They confirmed that one substance can be changed into another by rearranging their parts, just like Jabir ibn Hayyan had said, hundreds of years earlier.

什么物质能够促使这样的变化发生呢？他不知道，但他将其称为"al-iksir"，这是一个阿拉伯语单词。从这个单词演变出了如今的另一个单词"elixir"（灵丹妙药），指的是一种神奇的饮剂——我们可以在哈利·波特的故事乃至其他很多关于魔法的古老传说中找到这个词。

在过去的大部分世纪中，科学家对于任何能够将一种元素转变为另一种元素的方法持怀疑态度，认为这种转变是不可能的。

他们认为关于炼金术士或者巫师的故事都是"不科学的"。

1901年，有两位英国科学家在一所实验室中研究放射性金属。其中一位名叫弗雷德里克·索迪（Frederick Soddy），他注意到元素钍正在转变为元素镭。

他大声叫来了伙伴欧内斯特·卢瑟福（Ernest Rutherford）："卢瑟福，看！这就是转变！"

卢瑟福回答道："别把这叫作转变。他们会把我们当作炼金术士，砍下我们的脑袋。"

卢瑟福很担心其他科学家把他们当作想成为巫师的人，不再尊敬他们。

但这种情况并未发生。卢瑟福和索迪声名远扬。他们证实了一种物质可以通过结构改变而成为另一种物质，就像几百年前哈扬所说的那样。

---

① **skeptical** ['skeptɪkəl] *adj.* 怀疑的、怀疑论的、不可知的［more skeptical, most skeptical］

② **radioactive** [ˌreɪdɪəʊ'æktɪv] *adj.* 放射性的、有辐射的

③ **thorium** ['θɔːrɪəm] *n.* 钍（放射性金属元素，元素符号 Th，原子序数为 90）

④ **would-be** ['wudbiː] *adj.* 想要成为的、自称的、冒充的；*n.* 想要成为……人

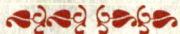

These days, scientists think the "philosopher's stone" is different from all other substances, and better thought of as a process, rather than a thing.

Diamonds are made by the crushing of carbon. Gold is made by the processes that happen in the center of stars.

So next time you read about an alchemist changing one thing into another, just remember that that is one subject on which scientists and wizards have (after many centuries) come to an agreement — the wizards were right!

如今，科学家认为"哲人石"和其他任何物质都不同，与其把它看作一种物质，不如把它当作一种加工方法。

钻石是通过挤压碳而形成的，金是恒星内部发生反应而形成的。

所以，下一次当你读到炼金术士将一种物质转变为另一种物质时，只要记住：在这个问题上科学家和巫师（在许多个世纪之后）达成了共识——巫师是正确的！

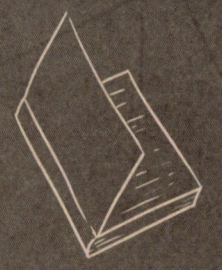

THE BULLIED BOY WHO FOUGHT BACK

艾萨克·牛顿
被欺负后还手的男孩

LITTLE ISAAC WAS BULLIED at school by a boy called Arthur. That's bad enough, but the story gets worse. His mother made him live with the **bully**①'s family, so he couldn't get away, but was stuck with him day and night, weekdays and weekends.

Isaac seemed to be a really unlucky boy. His father, a farmer, had died before he was born. His mother left him with relatives when he was three, because she had found a new husband.

You'd think that destiny would give a child with so many **disadvantages**② some good news to balance it out — but this seemed not to be the case. Well, not at first, anyway.

You see, fate also failed to give him much of a **personality**③. Isaac was no good at making friends. At school he sat by himself. Life was **miserable**④.

Now, all this happened in the UK in the 1600s, so a lonely child could not find friends the way modern youngsters do, through the Internet or youth clubs.

小男孩艾萨克在学校里被一个名叫亚瑟的男孩欺负了。这已经够糟糕的了,但接下来的事情更糟糕:艾萨克的母亲让他和亚瑟一家住在一起。他没法逃走,只能和亚瑟从早到晚日日夜夜待在一起。

艾萨克似乎是个很不幸的男孩。他的父亲是一名农场主,在他出生前就去世了。母亲在他三岁时改嫁,因此离开了艾萨克,把他托付给了亲戚。

你可能会以为,这个小孩这么不幸,为了平衡一下,上帝也许会带给他一些好运。但事实似乎并非如此,至少最初不是这样。

你会发现,他也没有天生的人见人爱的性格。他不擅长交友,在学校也是独自一人坐着。他的人生很悲惨。

这一切都发生在17世纪的英国,一个孤独的孩子不可能像现代的年轻人一样,通过网络或者青年俱乐部去交友。

---

① **bully** [ˈbʊlɪ] *n.* 欺凌弱小者、土霸; *vt.* 欺负、威吓; *vi.* 欺侮人
② **disadvantage** [dɪsədˈvɑːntɪdʒ] *n.* 缺点、不利条件、损失 [disadvantaged, disadvantaged, disadvantaging]
③ **personality** [pɜːsəˈnælɪtɪ] *n.* 个性、品格、名人 [personalities]
④ **miserable** [ˈmɪz(ə)rəb(ə)l] *adj.* 悲惨的、痛苦的、卑鄙的

So books became Isaac's main friends. He **naughtily**[①] scratched his name into the sill of the window at the school library as he sat there reading. His favorite books were the Bible and a science book called "The Mysteries of Nature and Art".

The bully, a boy called Arthur, was not just bigger and stronger than Isaac, but he was smart too — he was top of the class.

The lonely boy put up with the bullying for as long as he could, and then he got angry. "Beware the anger of the patient man," he read in his Bible.

Isaac took **revenge**[②]. First, he grabbed Arthur and slammed his face into the wall. And then he started speaking up at school — and stole Arthur's position as the smartest boy in school.

Soon, Isaac was **on a roll**[③]. He had an amazing brain, and he seemed to just get smarter and smarter.

Arthur's sister Catherine took a liking to the strange, unfriendly boy — and made a remarkable discovery.

He was not just reading about science. He was doing experiments and making things. In his room she saw a model **windmill**[④] that really worked, and a device that got its power from Isaac's pet mouse. He had also made a water clock. And he kept huge numbers of notes, in tiny writing, that no one else could read.

Isaac had invented his own language.

所以书成了艾萨克主要的伙伴。他调皮地在学校图书馆的窗台上刻下了自己的名字——他经常坐在那里看书。他最喜欢的是《圣经》和科学书刊《自然和艺术的秘密》。

那个名叫亚瑟的恃强凌弱者不仅比艾萨克魁梧，而且也很聪明——他是班上成绩最好的。

孤独的艾萨克已经忍受亚瑟的欺凌很久了，最终被彻底惹恼了。他在《圣经》中读到了这样的一句话："当心容忍者的暴怒。"

艾萨克开始了复仇。他抓住亚瑟，把他的脸猛按在墙上；后来在学校里也敢于畅所欲言——他取代亚瑟，成为学校里最聪明的男孩。

很快，艾萨克的好运来了。他有一个不可思议的大脑，看起来他似乎变得越来越聪明。

亚瑟的姐姐凯瑟琳（Catherine）开始喜欢这位举止奇怪且不太友善的男孩，并且有了一个惊人的发现。

艾萨克不只是阅读关于科学的书，他还做实验、制造东西。她在艾萨克的房间里看到了一个能够转动的风车模型，一个能从宠物鼠身上获取能量的装置……他甚至制作了一个水钟。他用其他人难以看懂的小字记下了大量的笔记。

艾萨克发明了他自己独特的语言。

---

① **naughtily** [ˈnɔtəli] *adv.* 顽皮地、无礼地
② **revenge** [rɪˈven(d)ʒ] *n.* 报复、复仇；*vt.* 报复、替……报仇、洗雪；*vi.* 报仇、雪耻 [revenged, revenged, revenging]
③ **on a roll** 运气好、超常发挥、做得很顺
④ **windmill** [ˈwɪn(d)mɪl] *n.* 风车、风车房、旋转玩具、直升机；*vt.* 使旋转；*vi.* 作风车般旋转

Well, you might have guessed who I am talking about. Isaac grew up to become the most famous scientist in history. Even super-brainy people like Einstein were **in awe of**① the discoveries of Sir Isaac Newton.

Being bullied is not nice — but it turned out to be the turning point in one child's life. And if you go to one school in the UK, you can still see a little piece of **vandalism**② by a frustrated child that has now become one of its greatest **treasures**③: the name "Isaac" scratched into the window sill of the school library.

你可能猜到我在谈论谁了。艾萨克长大后成为了历史上最著名的科学家。即使是像爱因斯坦这样的智者,也对艾萨克·牛顿爵士(Sir Isaac Newton)的发现敬佩不已。

被欺负不是件好事——但它成了那个孩子人生中的转折点。如果你去英国的那所学校,你仍然可以在图书馆窗台上看到刻下的名字"艾萨克"。这在当时是一个沮丧的孩子所作的小小的破坏行为,但现在已经成为那所学校最珍贵的财富之一。

① **in awe of** 恐惧、敬畏
② **vandalism** ['vænd(ə)lɪz(ə)m] *n.* 汪达尔人作风、故意毁坏文物的行为、破坏他人财产的行为
③ **treasure** ['treʒə] *n.* 财富、财产、财宝、珍品;*vt.* 珍爱、珍藏 [treasured , treasured , treasuring]

THE TEENAGER WHO SAW THE LIGHT

伽利略
观察吊灯的年轻人

A TEENAGE BOY WHO LEFT his studies for a break ended up making an important discovery.

When the famous scientist Galileo was just a teenager in Italy, he had to study hard, just like young people have to do today.

One day, when he was about 19, Galileo Galilei, who was very religious all his life (even after his famous argument with the **Pope**[1]!), decided to take a break from his books and go to church to pray.

He arrived there early, and sat in a **pew**[2] while watching staff get prepared for the service.

He watched the lamplighter arrive to do his job. Today, we use the word "**chandelier**[3]" to refer to a **cluster**[4] of electric lights hanging from the ceiling. But the word really means "lamp of candles", and in Galileo's time, a chandelier was filled with real candles lit with actual flames.

一个年轻人暂时离开书桌稍作休息，结果却作出了一个重大的发现。

　　意大利著名的科学家伽利略（Galileo Galilei）十几岁时，就像如今的年轻人一样，也不得不努力学习。

　　伽利略一生信奉宗教（即使在他与教皇进行了那场著名的争辩之后），大约在他19岁时的某一天，他决定暂时休息一下，放下书本，去教堂做礼拜。

　　他早早地来到教堂，坐在长凳上，看着工作人员准备礼拜的事宜。

　　他看着灯夫走进教堂开始干活。如今，我们用"枝形吊灯"这个词指代一串悬挂在天花板上的电灯，但这个词真正的含义是"插有蜡烛的灯"。在伽利略那个时代，一盏枝形吊灯上确实插满了正在燃烧的蜡烛。

① **Pope** [pəʊp] *n.* 教皇、罗马教皇
② **pew** [pjuː] *n.* 座位、教堂内的靠背长凳；*vt.* 排座位
③ **chandelier** [ˌʃændəˈlɪə] *n.* 枝形吊灯
④ **cluster** [ˈklʌstə] *n.* 群、簇、丛、串；*vi.* 群聚、丛生；*vt.* 使聚集、聚集在某人的周围

The lamplighter had two long sticks. He used one of them to hold the lamp **steady**[1] and the other to light a flame on each candle.

The young man noticed that when the lamplighter let go of the chandelier, it swung backwards and forwards. There was nothing strange about that.

But as the lamplighter continued his way down the aisle, lighting the lamps, something curious caught the boy's attention.

The lamps that swung a long distance each way swung quickly. The ones that swung a short distance swung slowly. The ones that swung a medium distance swung at a medium speed.

One of the most important things that scientists do is uncover "the laws of physics". These are the rules that form the **foundation**[2] of reality, and are of great interest to inventors and anyone who is interested in how reality works.

Galileo wondered if there was a law of physics here, making all the lamps swing the same distance in any given period of time, even though they seemed to be swinging different distances at different speeds.

灯夫手拿两根长棒，他用其中一根固定住灯，再用另一根点燃每一根蜡烛。

伽利略注意到，当灯夫松开固定灯的长棒时，灯会前后摇摆。这并不奇怪。

但当灯夫沿着走廊离开，继续点下一盏灯时，一个奇怪的现象吸引了伽利略的注意力。

那些摆动幅度大的吊灯摆速快，那些摆动幅度小的吊灯摆速慢，那些摆动幅度适中的吊灯摆速适中。

科学家最重要的工作之一是发现"物理学定律"，也就是构成现实基础的法则。对于发明家和任何对现实世界如何运转感兴趣的人来说，物理学定律非常有意思。

伽利略猜想，是否存在一条物理学定律，证明一盏吊灯总是在相同的时间内完成一次摆动，即使它看起来是以不同的速度摆过不同的距离？

---

① **steady** ['stedɪ] *adj.* 稳定的、不变的，沉着的；*vi.* 稳固；*vt.* 使稳定、稳固、使坚定；*adv.* 稳定地、稳固地 [steadier , steadiest , steadied , steadied, steadying]

② **foundation** [faʊn'deɪʃ(ə)n] *n.* 基础、地基

To find out for sure, the boy needed a clock.

But where would he find one?

The normal ways we find out the time, by looking at phones or **wristwatches**[1], were not available to him since this story took place in the 1500s.

He had an idea. He put two fingers on his wrist. He could feel his **pulse**[2] going throb, throb, throb, throb.

He used this regular beat as a clock to time the swings of the lamps, and found that his observations **confirmed**[3] his idea: a law of nature operated in the way objects swung from side to side, making them all match.

And so a teenage boy discovered a principle that turned out to be quite important, used all over the world in things such as pendulum clocks.

You're never too young to make a discovery!

为了验证这条定律，他需要一个时钟。

但他去哪里找到一个钟呢？

我们现在想知道准确时间，通常只要看手机或者手表就行了，但这个故事发生在 16 世纪，那时还没有这些东西呢！

他想到了一个主意。他把两根手指搭在手腕上，感受脉搏的跳动。

他将这种有规律的脉动当作时钟，测定吊灯的摆动时间。最后发现，他的观察证实了他的观点：一条自然法则以某种方式操纵着一个摆动的物体，使它从一边摆动到另一边、再回到原位所花的时间相同。

年轻的伽利略发现的这条定律最终被证实是非常重要的，它被应用于全世界像钟摆这样的物体上。

你永远不会因为太年轻而无法有所发现！

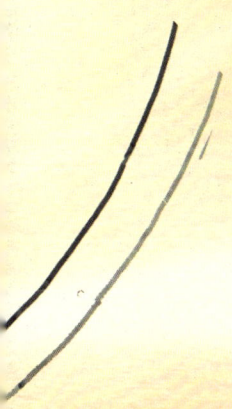

① **wristwatch** [ˈrɪs(t)wɒtʃ] *n.* 手表 [wristwatches]
② **pulse** [pʌls] *n.* 脉冲、脉搏；*vt.* 使跳动；*vi.* 跳动、脉动 [pulsed, pulsed, pulsing]
③ **confirm** [kənˈfɜːm] *vt.* 确认、确定、证实、批准、使巩固

WHAT WE LEARN FROM THE STRANGE TALE OF THE HUMAN COMPUTER

夏琨塔拉·德维
从人脑计算机的神奇传说中
得到的收获

ONCE THERE WAS a circus performer who **adored**[1] his baby girl.

During his working hours, he swung from dangerous **trapezes**[2], tamed lions, walked **tightropes**[3], and delighted crowds with his **magic tricks**[4].

But he couldn't wait for his free time, when he could spend time with his daughter.

When the girl, Shakuntala Devi, was three years old, her father taught her some tricks using cards.

He noticed that she had what seemed like a strange "**superpower**[5]"— she could memorize numbers and do calculations faster than any adult.

Of course, there were many adults who could do tricks with cards, or remember long numbers, but Shakuntala Devi's powers seemed remarkable. They really seemed super-human. Could it be so?

The circus life was tough. He worked hard but did not earn enough money to pay for school for the child or even enough to buy food for their meals.

Then he had an idea. He decided that the most amazing thing in the circus was actually outside the **circus ring**[6], in the humble tent where he lived: his daughter.

从前有一名马戏表演家,他非常喜欢自己的宝贝女儿。

　　工作期间,他在危险的秋千上摇摆、驯服狮子、走钢丝,用奇妙的表演逗乐观众。

　　但他渴望休息,在空闲时间陪伴女儿。

　　当女儿夏琨塔拉·戴维(Shakuntala Devi)三岁时,父亲教她一些用卡片玩的魔术。

　　他注意到,女儿戴维看起来拥有一种奇异的"超能力"——她可以迅速地记住数字并进行运算,比任何成年人都要快。

　　当然,很多成年人可以用卡片变魔术或者记住长串的数字,但夏琨塔拉·戴维的能力看起来非常不可思议,真的就像拥有超人才有的能力似的。这是真的吗?

✿✿✿✿✿

　　马戏团的生活很艰苦。这位父亲工作很努力,但挣的钱依然不够供戴维上学,甚至连每天的伙食费都不够。

　　不久他意识到,马戏团里最令人惊讶之物其实在马戏场外,在他住的那个简陋帐篷中:他的女儿。

---

① **adore** [əˈdɔː] vt. 崇拜、爱慕、喜爱、极喜欢;vi. 崇拜、爱慕 [adored,adored,adoring]
② **trapeze** [trəˈpiːz] n. 秋千、吊架
③ **tightrope** [ˈtaɪtrəʊp] n. 拉紧的绳索 [tightroped, tightroped, tightroping]
④ **magic tricks** 魔术
⑤ **superpower** [ˈsuːpəpaʊə; ˈsjuː-] n. 超能力,超级大国、超级强权
⑥ **circus ring** 马戏场

So the circus performer left his job and went on tour — charging people fees to see his amazing child do tricks with numbers.

They were not tricks. She really could do all sorts of things with her brain. You could make up any impossibly hard calculation, such as "What is 7,928,378,467 times 8,283,739,408?" and she would give you the answer, instantly, apparently without thinking.

She just seemed to know it. And when you checked with a calculator, she was always right!

Her fame spread far and wide. The family moved from their home in India to the UK when she entered her teens, and by the time she was 20, she was on tour in Europe as "the human computer".

Professors in the UK and the US tested the speed of her brain against computers, and she beat them every time.

In one experiment, a professor set her two extremely difficult problems to solve at once. "What is the cube **root**[1] of 61,629,875?" and "What is the seventh root of 170,859,375?"

Shakuntala Devi gave the right answers to both questions before the professor's wife had even started the timer.

Scientists began to realize that she was not a human computer — she was much faster than any computer.

所以这位马戏表演家辞掉了工作，开始进行巡回演出——让女儿表演那惊人的数字戏法，然后向观众收费。

他们并不是骗子。戴维确实可以运用她的大脑做任何事。你可以编造任何几乎不可能解答的困难算法，比如："7 928 378 467 和 8 283 739 408 相乘是多少？"，她能够立刻不假思索地告诉你答案。

她好像就是知道答案。你要是用计算器检验，会发现她总是正确的！

戴维声名远扬。当她十几岁时，他们一家从印度搬到了英国。20 岁时，她已经作为"人脑计算机"在欧洲巡演了。

英国和美国的教授对她的大脑运算速度和计算机的速度做对比测试，她每次都战胜了计算机。

在一次实验中，一位教授向她提出了两个特别难的问题："61 629 875 的立方根是多少？"，"170 859 375 的七次方根是多少？"要求立刻作答。

夏琨塔拉·戴维在教授的妻子开始计时前就给出了两个问题的正确答案。

科学家意识到，她不是人脑计算机——她的大脑运转得比任何计算机还要快！

---

① root [ruːt] n. 根、根源、词根、祖先；vi. 生根、根除；vt. 生根、固定、根源在于

You'd think that a person with a brain like this would have become a professor herself.

But remember, Shakuntala Devi had barely had any schooling, since her parents could not pay school fees.

And also her personality was a factor. She didn't want to become a professor. She came from a poor background and wanted to use her fame and powers to celebrate her love of humanity.

Shakuntala Devi became a writer of popular books. She wrote one of the first books in Asia arguing that society should be careful not to be hostile to **gay**[①] people.

She loved the mysteries of **mysticism**[②] and wrote books about the stars and **spirituality**[③], which she felt was a subject that the average person would find interesting and comforting. She also wrote novels and even cookbooks.

In this book, and in this series, we have focused mainly on scientists who discovered things.

But we are including this wonderful woman, who died in 2013, because although she was not a scientist herself, she was important to science.

你可能会认为有这样聪明头脑的人一定会成为一名教授。

但你得知道,她的父母付不起学费,所以夏琨塔拉·戴维几乎没有受过教育。

而且她的性格也是一个影响因素,她不想成为一名教授。她出身贫寒,想要用她的名望和能力去纪念人性中的爱。

夏琨塔拉·戴维成了一名畅销书作家。她在亚洲出版的第一本书,是第一批呼吁社会应该关爱而不是敌视同性恋的图书。

她爱上了神秘主义的神秘性,写了许多关于占星和灵性的书籍,她认为这是个能让一般人觉得有趣、轻松的话题。她也写小说,甚至编写食谱。

在这本乃至这个系列的书中,我们主要关注的是作出了新发现的科学家。

但我们也收录了这位杰出的女性,她在 2013 年去世。尽管她并不是一位科学家,却对科学作出了重要贡献。

---

① **gay** [geɪ] *n.* 同性恋者;*adj.* 快乐的、放荡的, 艳丽的 [gayer, gayest]
② **mysticism** [ˈmɪstɪsɪz(ə)m] *n.* 神秘、神秘主义, 谬论
③ **spirituality** [ˌspɪrɪtjʊˈælətɪ] *n.* 灵性、精神性 [spiritualities]

She established and demonstrated the amazing powers of the human brain — and the **over-riding**① importance of caring for the hopes and concerns of ordinary people.

People are starting to realize that the human brain is not really just a very good computer, but a completely different type of thing altogether. It's an intriguing thought, and shows that whatever new devices scientists and technologists throw up, none of them is ever likely to be as powerful and magical and **unique**② as the human mind.

她拥有并且展示了人类大脑的惊人能力——以及关怀普通人的希望和忧虑的重要性。

人们开始意识到，人类的大脑并不仅仅是一台优秀的计算机，它是与计算机截然不同的物体。大脑拥有着错综复杂的思维，这也表明：无论科学家和技术专家制造出什么新的仪器，都不可能像人类大脑一样强大、精妙、独一无二。

① **over-riding** [ˌəʊvəˈraɪdɪŋ] *adj.* 高于一切的、最重要的
② **unique** [juːˈniːk] *adj.* 独特的、稀罕的、唯一的、独一无二的；*n.* 独一无二的人或物

The Young Scientists Series:
Women of Discovery and The Mystery of Nature Laws

by

Nury Vittachi

English Copyright © 2017 by World Scientific Publishing Co. Pte. Ltd.

Bi-lingual (Simplified Chinese & English) Character Copyright © 2018 by Shanghai Scientific & Technological Education Publishing House

Shanghai Scientific & Technological Education Publishing House published bi-lingual edition by arranged with World Scientific Publishing Co. Pte. Ltd., Singapore

All rights reserved. This book, or parts thereof, may not be reproduced in any form or by any means, electronic or mechanical, including photocopying, recording or any information storage and retrieval system now known or to be invented, without written permission from the Publisher.

ALL RIGHTS RESERVED
上海科技教育出版社业经World Scientific Publishing Co. Pte. Ltd.同意
取得本书中英文双语版版权

责任编辑　侯慧菊
封面设计　杨　静

"伟人的少年故事"丛书
突破障碍的人——改写了科学史的伟大人物
[斯里兰卡]努雷·维塔奇（Nury Vittachi）　著
斯泰帕·张（Step Cheung）　图
朱之翀　译
张　群　审校

出版发行	上海科技教育出版社有限公司
	（上海市柳州路218号　邮政编码200235）
网　　址	www.ewen.co　www.sste.com
经　　销	各地新华书店
印　　刷	上海昌鑫龙印务有限公司
开　　本	889×1194　1/32
印　　张	3
版　　次	2018年8月第1版
印　　次	2018年8月第1次印刷
书　　号	ISBN 978-7-5428-6706-3/G·3832
图　　字	09-2017-937号
定　　价	25.00元

扫描二维码
获取教师参考资料
及练习答案

扫描二维码
获取学生练习册